Childcare Worker

CAREERS WITH CHARACTER

Career Assessments & Their Meaning
Childcare Worker
Clergy
Computer Programmer
Financial Advisor
Firefighter
Homeland Security Officer
Journalist
Manager
Military & Elite Forces Officer
Nurse
Politician
Professional Athlete & Sports Official
Psychologist
Research Scientist
Social Worker
Special Education Teacher
Veterinarian

CAREERS WITH CHARACTER

Childcare Worker

Ellyn Sanna

Mason Crest

Mason Crest
450 Parkway Drive, Suite D
Broomall, PA 19008
www.masoncrest.com

Printed in the Hashemite Kingdom of Jordan.

First printing
9 8 7 6 5 4 3 2 1

Series ISBN: 978-1-4222-2750-3
ISBN: 978-1-4222-2752-7
ebook ISBN: 978-1-4222-9048-4

The Library of Congress has cataloged the
hardcopy format(s) as follows:

Library of Congress Cataloging-in-Publication Data

Sanna, Ellyn, 1957-
  Childcare worker / Ellyn Sanna.
    pages cm. - (Careers with characters)
  Includes index.
    ISBN 978-1-4222-2752-7 (hardcover) - ISBN 978-1-4222-2750-3 (series) - ISBN 978-1-4222-9048-4 (ebook)
  1. Child care workers–Juvenile literature. 2. Child care services–Vocational guidance–Juvenile literature. I. Title.
  HQ778.5.S33 2014
  362.71'2–dc23
                          2013007675

Produced by Vestal Creative Services.
www.vestalcreative.com

Photo Credits:
Comstock: pp. 16, 26, 30, 32, 53, 63, 80, 81, 82, 84
PhotoDisc: pp. 10, 12, 13, 14, 19, 22, 24, 25, 27, 34, 37, 40, 42, 43, 44, 46, 48, 50, 52, 56, 58, 59, 60, 61, 62, 66, 68, 69, 70, 72, 73, 76, 78, 86, 88
Viola Ruelke Gommer: pp. 33, 36, 51

The individuals in these images are models, and the images are for illustrative purposes only. To the best knowledge of the publisher, all other images are in the public domain. If any image has been inadvertantly uncredited or miscredited, please notify Vestal Creative Services, Vestal, New York 13850, so that rectification can be made for future printings.

Contents

We each leave a fingerprint on the world.
Our careers are the work we do in life.
Our characters are shaped by the choices
we make to do good.
When we combine careers with character,
we touch the world with power.

Introduction

by Dr. Cheryl Gholar
and Dr. Ernestine G. Riggs

In today's world, the awesome task of choosing or staying in a career has become more involved than one would ever have imagined in past decades. Whether the job market is robust or the demand for workers is sluggish, the need for top-performing employees with good character remains a priority on most employers' lists of "must have" or "must keep." When critical decisions are being made regarding a company or organization's growth or future, job performance and work ethic are often the determining factors as to who will remain employed and who will not.

How does one achieve success in one's career and in life? Victor Frankl, the Austrian psychologist, summarized the concept of success in the preface to his book *Man's Search for Meaning* as: "The unintended side-effect of one's personal dedication to a course greater than oneself." Achieving value by responding to life and careers from higher levels of knowing and being is a specific goal of teaching and learning in "Careers with Character." What constitutes success for us as individuals can be found deep within our belief system. Seeking, preparing, and attaining an excellent career that aligns with our personality is an outstanding goal. However, an excellent career augmented by exemplary character is a visible expression of the human need to bring meaning, purpose, and value to our work.

Career education informs us of employment opportunities, occupational outlooks, earnings, and preparation needed to perform certain tasks. Character education provides insight into how a person of good character might choose to respond, initiate an action, or perform specific tasks in the presence of an ethical dilemma. "Careers with Character" combines the two and teaches students that careers are more than just jobs. Career development is incomplete without character development. What better way to explore careers and character than to make them a single package to be opened, examined, and reflected upon as a means of understanding the greater whole of who we are and what work can mean when one chooses to become an employee of character?

Character can be defined simply as "who you are even when no one else is around." Your character is revealed by your choices and actions. These bear your personal signature, validating the story of who you are. They are the fingerprints you leave behind on the people you meet and know; they are the ideas you bring into reality. Your choices tell the world what you truly believe.

Character, when viewed as a standard of excellence, reminds us to ask ourselves when choosing a career: "Why this particular career, for what purpose, and to what end?" The authors of "Careers with Character" knowledgeably and passionately, through their various vignettes, enable one to experience an inner journey that is both intellectual and moral. Students will find themselves, when confronting decisions in real life, more prepared, having had experiential learning opportunities through this series. The books, however, do not separate or negate the individual good from the academic skills or intellect needed to perform the required tasks that lead to productive career development and personal fulfillment.

Each book is replete with exemplary role models, practical strategies, instructional tools, and applications. In each volume, individuals of character work toward ethical leadership, learning how to respond appropriately to issues of not only right versus wrong, but issues of right versus right, understanding the possible benefits and consequences of their decisions. A wealth of examples is provided.

What is it about a career that moves our hearts and minds toward fulfilling a dream? It is our character. The truest approach to finding out who we are and what illuminates our lives is to look within. At the very heart of career development is good character. At the heart of good character is an individual who knows and loves the good, and seeks to share the good with others. By exploring careers and character together, we create internal and external environments that support and enhance each other, challenging students to lead conscious lives of personal quality and true richness every day.

Is there a difference between doing the right thing, and doing things right? Career questions ask, "What do you know about a specific career?" Character questions ask, "Now that you know about a specific career, what will you choose to do with what you know?" "How will you perform certain tasks and services for others, even when no one else is around?" "Will all individuals be given your best regardless of their socioeconomic background, physical condition, ethnicity, or religious beliefs?" Character questions often challenge the authenticity of what we say we believe and value in the workplace and in our personal lives.

Character and career questions together challenge us to pay attention to our lives and not fall asleep on the job. Career knowledge, self-knowledge, and ethical wisdom help us answer deeper questions about the meaning of work; they give us permission to transform our lives. Personal integrity is the price of admission.

The insight of one "ordinary" individual can make a difference in the world—if that one individual believes that character is an amazing gift to uncap knowledge and talents to empower the human community. Our world needs everyday heroes in the workplace—and "Careers with Character" challenges students to become those heroes.

Childcare workers provide children with safe, cheerful places to spend their days.

JOB REQUIREMENTS

*It takes more than an education
to be a good worker.*

CHAPTER ONE

Playing with children all day is a fun way to make a living. But imagine it's Friday afternoon, and all week you've been caring for a group of ten children. You've modeled funny animals out of clay; you've oohed and ahhed over finger-painted pictures; and you've sung silly songs and read out loud until your voice is tired. As you look back over your day, you realize you were playing patty-cake one minute and creating curriculum goals with your supervisor the next. You're tired—but the ten children for whom you are responsible are still going strong. You'd like to flop down and put your feet up. Instead, you're giving piggyback rides around the room. You love your job, and you love the children in your room, but

A childcare worker has the chance to play during every work-day.

sometimes you can't help but wonder: Do you have what it takes to be a long-term success as a childcare worker?

The training and credentials required of childcare workers vary across the United States and Canada. Depending on the childcare setting, job requirements can range from a high school diploma to community college courses to a bachelor's degree in child develop-ment or early-childhood education. Many states require continuing education for workers employed in this field, but other states have only minimal requirements.

Local governments, *private* organizations, and publicly funded programs may require more demanding training and education. Some employers in this field prefer to hire workers who have earned a nationally recognized childcare development credential or who at least have attended secondary or even post-secondary courses in child development and education. An increasing number of employers want to hire childcare workers who have at least an *associate's degree* in early-childhood education. There are even special schools for nannies, where these workers can learn how to deliver quality education, nutrition, and care to their charges.

According to the Occupational Handbook, about thirty percent of childcare workers were self-employed in 2010. Most of these workers are family childcare providers. This means they are paid directly by the children's parents or guardians, rather than working for a school or other organization.

In most cases, however, childcare workers can get a job if they have a high school diploma and a little experience. Chances are,

Some after-school programs may provide children with computers for games and learning.

you may already have some experience in this field, whether you've had a formal job or not. If you have ever done any babysitting, or if you even have younger brothers and sisters, then you will have accumulated experiences and skills on which you can build. Working as a camp counselor, volunteering to help out in your church nursery, or teaching a Sunday school class of younger children are also good ways to gain experience with children.

If you have already had an opportunity to take care of children, then you probably know you need some special qualities to work with young kids. College degrees and training programs are good, and they may be very helpful in helping you advance in your career—but even more important are the character and personality you bring to your work.

Childcare workers make sure children's nutritional needs are being met during the time children are under their care.

Childcare workers who work in private households are often called nannies. They bathe, dress, and feed very young children; they supervise their play, wash their clothes, and clean their rooms. They may also read to children and even teach them, and they often drive them to doctor's appointments and to other activities. Those who are in charge of infants will prepare bottles and change diapers. Nannies often live in the household, with their own room or apartment. They may perform the duties of a general housekeeper as well.

Your personality tends to be the collection of characteristics you either inherited genetically from your parents or you learned as you grew up in your unique environment. As a childcare worker, you will find that a specific kind of personality will help you be more successful as you work with young children. For instance, these workers need to be enthusiastic and energetic; they need to have the physical and emotional stamina to keep up with young children. They need to be constantly alert, in order to anticipate and prevent discipline and safety problems. Skills in music, art, drama, and storytelling, although not essential, will make the care these workers provide more interesting to young children.

Childcare workers also need to be able to communicate well. Although they spend most of their day working with children, they

To ensure that children receive proper supervision, state or local regulations may require certain ratios of workers to children. This ratio varies with the age of the children. Child development experts usually recommend that a single caregiver be responsible for no more than three or four babies (less than a year old), five or six toddlers (one to two years old), or ten preschool-age children (between two and five years old). In before- and after-school programs, workers may be responsible for many school-age children at a time.

In wealthy homes, live-in servants once provided childcare.

The History of Childcare

For centuries, children were cared for in their own homes by family members or by family servants. In the mid-1700s, however, many women in England began working in factories. If these women had no older children or other relatives to watch their young children, they usually had to bring their small children to work with them. This created a safety hazard, and some factory owners established special rooms for their workers' children. Unskilled workers were hired to watch the children while their parents were working in the factory. These were the first childcare centers. The first such facility was not established in the United States until a hundred years later when American women joined the workforce as manufacturing became a major industry.

will need to maintain contact with parents or guardians through informal meetings or scheduled conferences. Parents expect child-care workers to act as "temporary parents," and parents may often feel conflicted and anxious that they are unable to provide this care themselves; in order to feel that they are still involved with their children's lives during the time when they cannot be with them, they will want to be informed about their children's progress and updated on any problems or special needs. Many childcare workers keep records of each child's progress and suggest ways that parents can increase their children's learning and development at home. These workers try to work as a team with the parents; some preschools, childcare centers, and before- and after-school programs actively recruit parents to be volunteers in their programs. This means that as a childcare worker, you need to be prepared to communicate effectively with adults as well as children. Good communication skills are another part of the personality you'll need to succeed as a childcare worker.

If you want to take care of children for your living, you will also need the right character. The job requires the patience and self-

The working hours for this career vary widely. Childcare centers are open year round, with long hours so parents can drop off and pick up their children before and after work. Some centers employ full-time and part-time workers to cover the entire day with staggered shifts. In childcare centers where funds are lacking, the limited staffing may mean that workers are unable to take regular breaks. Preschool programs (both *public* and private) usually operate only during the nine- or ten-month school year; they often employ both full- and part-time workers. Childcare workers employed by private families usually have flexible schedules, but they may work long or unusual hours to accommodate the parents' work routines. Live-in nannies usually work longer hours than those who have their own homes, but if they work evenings or weekends, they are usually given other free time.

A childcare worker needs to be sensitive to each child's unique needs.

discipline necessary to read the same story four times in a row; it demands the compassion and respect needed to treat each child with tenderness; and it asks that you be responsible enough that parents can trust their children to you. All these traits are necessary to a childcare worker's character.

Your character is different from your personality. Unlike your personality, which may be the result of forces beyond your control, your character is who *you* choose to be. Each time you decide how to act in any given situation, you are also deciding the sort of character you want to have. When you decide to do right, you shape your character in one direction—and when you select the alternative that is morally wrong, you mold your character in an entirely different way. These moments of decision are often called *ethical dilemmas.*

Each of us, no matter how old we are or what career we choose for ourselves, will inevitably face these dilemmas throughout our lives.

According to character education expert Tom Lickona, good character depends on possessing certain core qualities. We've already mentioned a few of these, qualities like self-discipline, compassion, and respect. Other aspects of a good character include integrity and trustworthiness, justice and fairness, and citizenship. These values are important to who we are—and they are important to our society as a whole. They not only make us happier individuals, but they also serve the common good. When we demonstrate these qualities in our lives, then we treat others the way we would like to be treated.

As a childcare worker, this means you will need to remember what it felt like to be three years old, living in a world where the

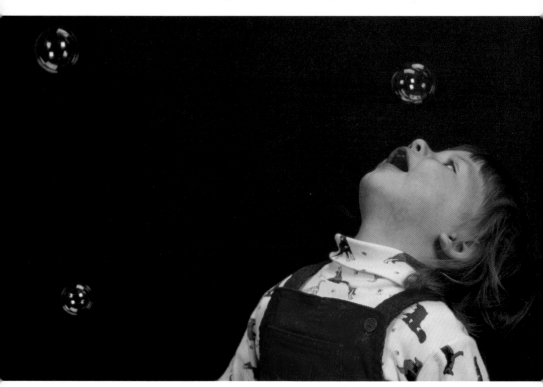

Taking care of children offers many opportunities for joy.

Professional Organizations for Childcare Workers

The National Association of Child Care Professionals (NACCP) serves the directors, administrators, and owners of childcare facilities. The organization's goal is to encourage the management sector of childcare to possess a strong set of child development skills and a powerful collection of core management competencies. They believe that without this combination of abilities, superior childcare is impossible.

The National Association for the Education of Young Children (NAEYC) is dedicated to improving the quality of programs for children from birth through third grade. Founded in 1926, the NAEYC has over 100,000 members and a national network of nearly 450 local, state, and regional *affiliates*. Affiliate groups work to improve professional practice and working conditions in early childhood education and to build public support for high-quality early childhood programs.

The **National Association for Family Child Care** is a nonprofit organization dedicated to promoting quality childcare. Its goals are:

1. To strengthen state and local associations as support systems for individual childcare providers.
2. To promote a professional accreditation program that encourages quality childcare.
3. To represent childcare providers by advocating for their needs and collaborating with other organizations.
4. To promote the diversity of the childcare profession through training, state and local associations, public education, and board membership.
5. To deliver effective programs through strong organizational management.

grownups towered over you. You will respect children's individuality and not take advantage of your own power. And you will think of their parents' perspective as well, often asking yourself this question: If these were your own children, how would you want them to be treated by their childcare worker?

In the chapters that follow, we will look at the ethical dilemmas faced by childcare workers, and we will see how the following character traits are played out in their careers:

- Integrity and trustworthiness
- Respect and compassion
- Justice and fairness
- Responsibility
- Courage
- Self-discipline and diligence
- Citizenship

It takes a village to raise a child.

—African proverb

Some childcare workers live in a family's home and care for the children when the parents are away.

INTEGRITY AND TRUSTWORTHINESS

Your character is worth more than any amount of money.

CHAPTER TWO

Ritesh Patel was excited about his life. He had dreams and goals for the future—and in the meantime he had a job he loved. But he nearly lost everything when he failed to act with integrity in his role as childcare worker.

Ritesh worked as a live-in childcare provider for a well-to-do family in Toronto, Canada. He enjoyed spending time during the day with the family's eleven-month-old baby and three-year-old daughter. His evenings were his own, and he was attending as many night classes as he could at a local university. One day, when he had saved enough money, he hoped to go to medical school full time so that he could become a *pediatrician.* Ritesh loved children, and he was excited about both his present and future careers.

When Mr. and Mrs. Sze-tu left for work each morning, they knew their children were in good hands. Ritesh would be there when the children woke up; he would make them laugh while he prepared their breakfasts, and then he would get them dressed. They would spend their morning playing in the park if the weather was good, or painting and playing games in the house if the weather was bad. At noon, he would give the children their lunches, and then he would read to them and settle them down for their naps. The Sze-tus knew their children loved hearing Ritesh play on his guitar as they fell asleep. Both Mr. and Mrs. Sze-tu felt that Ritesh was an important part of their family's life; neither of them could have enjoyed their professional lives as much if they had not been so confident that their children were being lovingly cared for by Ritesh.

Childcare workers take over many of a parent's responsibilities —including teaching children beginning reading skills.

Since childcare workers are in effect "substitute parents," they need to offer children plenty of love and attention.

Ritesh had only worked for the Sze-tus for three months, but he already felt as though he were almost part of the family. He understood that the Sze-tus depended on him to keep their children safe and happy. He valued their trust, and he had no intention of ever letting them down.

But one day while the children were napping, as Ritesh was straightening up the living room, he found something: a hundred-dollar bill had slipped between the sofa cushions. The phone rang just as he found it, and without thinking, Ritesh slid the bill into his pocket.

Later that evening, while Ritesh was out at a restaurant with some friends, he reached into his pocket to pay for his meal—and pulled

Whatever career field you choose, you will need to be clear about your priorities. Is money the most important thing—or are principles like integrity and honesty?

out the hundred-dollar bill. He put it quickly back into his pocket, intending to give it to the Sze-tus when he got back to their house.

But as he drove home, he began to think about that one hundred dollars. The Sze-tus were very wealthy; losing a hundred-dollar bill for them was probably like losing a five-dollar bill would be for him. They would barely even notice that it was missing—and they would have no way of knowing he had found it. Although the Sze-tus paid him generously, a hundred dollars was a lot of money for him. He did his job well, and he would never do anything that would endanger the Sze-tu children in any way. Maybe he should just look at the hundred dollars as an unexpected windfall, a sort of bonus for all his hard work. He could tuck it away in the account where he kept his savings for medical school . . . or he could use it for a fun date with his girlfriend.

One way to solve an ethical dilemma is to use the technique that Ritesh did: Imagine that whatever choice you make will be broadcast as the headline in a newspaper. How would you feel if the whole world knew your decision? How would you feel if your mother knew? Or if the children in your life were aware of the choice you had made?

If your answer to this question makes you feel uncomfortable, ashamed, or embarrassed, chances are you are not making a moral decision. When we choose to act with integrity, we do not need to be afraid that others will find out what we have done. We can hold our heads high, knowing we have done the right thing.

Solving an ethical dilemma is never easy. Although you may seek advice from others, ultimately, only you can make up your mind about what is the right thing to do.

28

By the time he reached the Sze-tus' home, Ritesh had decided to keep the money. He went straight to his room, without speaking to either Mr. or Mrs. Sze-tu. As he got ready to go to bed, he had no way of knowing that the Sze-tus were talking about him in their room down the hall.

"The money is gone," Mrs. Sze-tu said, her voice heavy.

"Maybe one of the children found it," her husband answered. "Who knows? You never should have tried such a stupid test. Now we'll feel uneasy about Ritesh—and he may not have taken the money. I wish you hadn't listened to that woman at work."

Mrs. Sze-tu nodded. "But she seemed to make sense. She says she always tests her household employees so she doesn't have to worry about whether they're trustworthy or not. We know Ritesh is good with the children. But do we really know we can trust him in our home when we're not here? He's only worked for us for a few months, and I've been careful to keep my jewelry put away out of sight. But what if he searches the house while we're not here? I don't want to feel like I have to take an inventory every time I come home, to make sure nothing's missing."

Mr. Sze-tu sighed. "I don't think we should be so suspicious. He's given us no reason to mistrust him."

"Then where's the money?"

The Sze-tus looked at each other for a long moment. "Maybe we should think about hiring someone else," Mr. Sze-tu said finally. "We can't have a thief in our home, no matter how much the children love him. We'll talk to the children first and see if they found the money. And then, if they don't have it, we'll have to find someone to take his place."

Ritesh woke up early the next morning. Something was making him uneasy. After a moment, he remembered the hundred dollars he had found the day before.

He had made excuses to himself for keeping the money, but now he found himself wondering: How would he feel if the children knew he had taken the money? Or what if his mother knew? The thought made his stomach turn over. He knew what his mother would say.

As he showered, he imagined a newspaper headline proclaiming to all the world: RITESH PATEL STEALS $100 FROM EMPLOYER. The mental image made him squirm. He could be expelled from the university for something like this, and all his dreams for the future would be destroyed.

But even if no one ever discovered what he had done, *he* would know. He didn't want to live with a secret like that. A hundred dollars simply wasn't worth the cost to his character. A million dollars wouldn't be worth it, he realized.

He got dressed, and then he found the hundred-dollar bill in the pocket of the pants he had worn the day before. "Mrs. Sze-tu," he called, hurrying down the hallway to catch her before she left for work. "I found something of yours yesterday. I should have returned it last night. Please forgive me."

Mrs. Sze-tu's eyes searched his face. Then she smiled and reached for the money. "Thank you, Ritesh."

A spirit of selfishness destroys the bonds that unite us, but integrity builds trust.

—Mason George Snapp

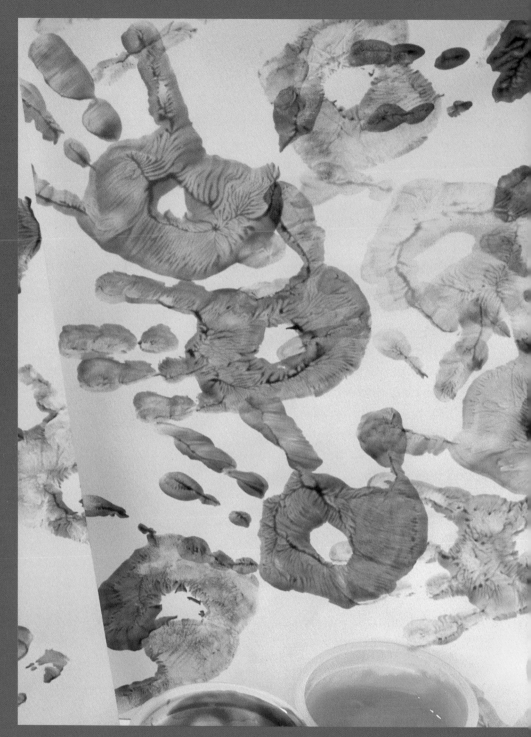

Children enjoy opportunities to express themselves creatively.

RESPECT AND COMPASSION

Children don't have to earn our respect and compassion—they deserve it simply because they exist.

CHAPTER THREE

Every day, Molly Barton has plenty of opportunities to show respect and compassion. The constant challenge to demonstrate these character qualities is a part of her daily life.

Molly runs a daycare facility out of her home in a small town in Ohio. As the mother of her own young child, she is grateful for a career that allows her to work out of her home and be with her daughter. She enjoys spending time with young children, and she has come to care about each of her young charges.

After the parents drop off their children in the morning, Molly begins each day with a story. The children are usually quiet and a

Childcare workers should provide children with plenty of chances to learn through playing.

little sleepy during this time; some of them are still in their pajamas, since their parents were in a hurry to get to work and didn't have time to dress them. Molly knows that grown-up hustle and rush can be stressful for young children, and she tries to settle her group by reading to them with a soothing, cheerful voice.

By the time she has finished reading, the children are ready to begin play. Molly's daughter Rebecca and her friend Jacob usually head straight for the kitchen set, where they pretend to cook supper with the pots and pans. Little Jessie settles down to play with the brightly colored stacking toy. Nicholas and Terrell begin to color, and Samantha and Scott try on the dress-up clothes. Molly has found that the children will usually play happily for nearly an hour, and she uses this time to have a cup of coffee while she takes care of some bookkeeping chores.

Some mornings, however, things don't go quite so smoothly. For instance, one day last week Molly had a headache because she had been up in the night with Rebecca, who had had a bad dream. Molly felt cranky and tired, and she was longing for a peaceful morning—but just as she sat back to drink her coffee, she noticed that Samantha and Scott were arguing over who was going to wear the gypsy outfit.

When you have respect and compassion for others...

- you practice the Golden Rule. In other words, you treat other people the way you would like to be treated.
- you don't take advantage of situations in ways that might benefit you but hurt others.
- you demonstrate your concern for others.

You don't need to spend a lot of money to give children the chance to use their imaginations. With a little creativity, paper plates can turn into silly masks, offering kids many happy moments.

Interaction with peers is an important part of a child's early development. Childcare workers often structure opportunities for conversation and discussions. As they teach children to play and work cooperatively with their classmates, they play a vital role in preparing youngsters for school.

Molly sat quietly, listening, waiting to see if the two children would be able to settle their argument on their own. Respect for one another was an important part of what she tried to teach the children, and she was hoping Samantha and Scott would be able to use the skills she had tried to give them for resolving an argument. She soon realized, however, that the two children needed some help.

A good daycare facility allows children to learn about the world through playing with water, sand, and other materials.

Ten Childcare Commandments

1. Give continuous, consistent loving care. It's as necessary to a child's mental health as food is for the body.
2. Give generously of your time and understanding. Playing with and reading to a child matters far more than a neat, smooth-running home.
3. Provide new experiences and immerse the child in language from birth onward. This will enrich the child's growing mind.
4. Encourage the child to play, both alone and with others. Exploring, imitating, constructing, pretending, and creating should be the occupations of every child.
5. Praise more for effort than for achievement.
6. Give a child ever-increasing responsibilities; like all skills, responsibility needs to be practiced.
7. Remember that every child is unique. What's suitable for one child may not be right for another.
8. Show your disapproval in a way that fits the individual child's temperament, age, and level of understanding.
9. Disapprove of behaviors—not the child. Never suggest to a child that your love is conditional upon good behavior.
10. Don't expect gratitude for your care. Children have the right to expect adults to take care of them. They did not ask to be put upon this earth.

Adapted from Mia Kellmer Pringle's *The Needs of Children*.

As a childcare worker, you may learn as much as the child does.

"Mine!" Samantha insisted.

"You had it last time!" Scott protested. He grabbed hold of a brightly colored scarf and pulled it out of Samantha's hands. Samantha squealed and tugged it back.

With a sigh, Molly got to her feet and went to intervene.

She was tempted to scoop up the dress-up clothes, stuff them back in their box, and carry the box into the other room. After all, if Samantha and Scott couldn't play with the clothes appropriately, then they didn't deserve to play with them at all. That would be the easiest solution, the one that would allow Molly to return to her coffee most quickly.

But would that action be the kindest one on her part? Would she be showing the two children the same respect she wanted them to demonstrate to each other? Or would she be taking advantage of her power as the adult?

We seldom have a long time to consider when we are confronted with one of life's ethical dilemmas, and Molly had to make up her mind quickly. Because she truly cared about the two children, she decided to use this small incident as an opportunity for a learning experience.

Setting her coffee cup out of the reach of small hands, Molly sat down on the floor so she would be on level with Samantha and Scott. She asked them to take turns explaining the situation—and then she encouraged them to think what they should do next.

"He should give me the gypsy clothes," Samantha insisted. "They're girl clothes anyway."

Scott stuck out his lip. "I want to wear the gypsy clothes."

"But if you're fighting, then you're not having fun," Molly reminded them. "How can you work this out so you get back to playing?"

The two children stared at each other, neither one of them willing to back down. "I guess he could wear the scarf and the shirt," Samantha said at last. "And I could wear the skirt and the shawl. That way he could be a boy gypsy and I could be the girl gypsy."

Children in daycare facilities learn a vital life skill—how to get along with one another.

Five Steps for Making an Ethical Decision

1. *Clarify.* Determine what must be decided and list your options. Molly could have simply removed the dress-up clothes from the room—or she could take time to help the children find their own resolution.
2. *Evaluate.* See what character values are involved in your options. Consider the benefits and risks to everyone concerned. If Molly took the dress-up clothes away, the benefit to herself would be that she could return to her chair and coffee more quickly; the risk would be, however, that she might show the children that so long as you are bigger, you can do whatever you want. She would not have shown them that conflict can be resolved by working out alternatives.
3. *Decide.* Make sure your decision supports the Golden Rule. How would you want to be treated in the same situation?
4. *Implement.* Develop a plan to carry out your decision in such a way that benefits are maximized and risks minimized. As in Molly's case, you may not have a long time to develop a formal plan—but you can come up with a course of action that will support character values.
5. *Monitor and modify.* Keep an eye on the consequences of your decision as they unfold. Be willing to revise your plan—or scrap it altogether—if circumstances warrant. If Samantha and Scott had been unwilling to compromise, Molly might have had to eventually remove the clothes after all. Or a few minutes later, they might again begin to argue over the clothes, and Molly would have to intervene once more.

Scott agreed, and in a few minutes the children were happily pretending to be gypsies. Molly went back to her coffee with a grateful sigh.

As she sat down behind her desk, she smiled ruefully. When the children's parents left them each morning, the parents always told their children to "be good." Some days, she realized, "being good" was as much a challenge for her as it was for the little ones. Her head still hurt and she was still tired—but she was glad she had made the extra effort to show respect and compassion to Scott and Samantha.

We may not always see eye to eye, but we can try to see heart to heart.

—Sam Levenson

Before- and after-school programs provide children with a safe environment where they can learn, play, and interact.

JUSTICE
AND FAIRNESS

*All children have the right to a fair and
just world ... and it's up to adults to
make sure they get it.*

CHAPTER FOUR

Barbara Toto always tried to treat each one of the children the same. As a worker in the Blueridge Before- and After-School Program, she was responsible for overseeing a room full of school-age children from six to eight-thirty in the morning and from two-thirty until seven at night. The children all arrived in the morning and left in the afternoon at different times. Many of the children were tired and out of sorts during the hours they were with her, but she still enjoyed the chance to spend time with them. She had always wanted a career in childcare, and she welcomed the opportunity to help kids learn to get along better in life. Each one of the children

People who value justice and fairness:

- treat all people the same (as much as possible).
- are open-minded; they are willing to try to understand others' points of view.
- consider carefully before making decisions that affect others.
- recognize the uniqueness and value of each individual.

charactercounts.org/overview/about.html

she saw was unique and special, and Barbara worked hard to make the children see each other the same way.

Lately, though, Barbara had been having problems with one child, a fifth-grader named Abby Kolatch. Abby was bigger than the other kids in the room, and Barbara had

After-school programs give students a chance to work on homework.

More and more children go home from school while their parents are still at work.

Parents' concern over school-age children being home alone before and after school has spurred many families to seek out other alternatives. Before- and after-school programs are designed to fill the gap between children's school day and parents' workday. These programs may also operate all day during the summer and on weekends. Some facilities are even beginning to offer overnight care, for parents who work night shifts.

These before- and after-school programs are usually run by public school systems, local community centers, or churches and other private organizations. Workers in these programs may help students with their homework or keep them busy with extracurricular activities like field trips, learning about computers, sports, artwork, photography, or music.

Many after-school programs also include a time for sports.

noticed that the younger children were afraid of her. If Abby didn't get the art materials or game that she preferred, she would sometimes shove other children out of her way and take what she wanted by force. Barbara was getting fed up with Abby's belligerent attitude. Besides, Abby was an unattractive child; her clothes were always dirty, her hair unkempt, and her face wore a perpetual scowl.

So when Barbara saw Abby knock little Michael Parker on the floor one morning, Barbara was ready to take action. She grabbed Abby by the arm and marched her into a quiet corner of the room. "You and I need to talk," she hissed.

For a moment, Abby looked frightened, but then she stuck out her chin and shrugged. "So talk," she sneered.

Barbara took a deep breath. If she were honest with herself, she had to admit she was tempted to slap the girl across the face.

Physical punishment was out of the question, of course; even if Barbara had believed in hitting a child—which she didn't—such an action could cost her her job. But something in Abby's face made Barbara think she *expected* Barbara to hit her. She looked almost as though she were bracing herself for the blow.

Abby wasn't as cute as the other children. She never drew pictures for Barbara or brought her little gifts like the other kids did sometimes. Barbara didn't even particularly like the girl.

Despite all that, Abby deserved Barbara's care just as much as any of the children. If Barbara wanted to be fair, she needed to give her full attention to solving the dilemma with which she was faced. How should she handle Abby's behavior problem in a way that would demonstrate justice?

Barbara raised her hand and placed it on Abby's shoulder. The girl flinched. "Abby," Barbara said slowly, "did you think I was going to hit you?"

In 1972, Donna J. Stone established Prevent Child Abuse America, an organization dedicated to preventing all forms of child abuse. Donna believed that all adults need to work together to provide children with a safe and nurturing environment in which to grow.

Her first step was to educate and inform the public about the effects of child abuse. After overcoming numerous challenges, she convinced the Advertising Council to launch a nationwide campaign to end child abuse.

The results of her organization's efforts have been dramatic. The public's general awareness of this problem has increased from less than 10 percent in 1976 to well over 90 percent today. People also have a greater understanding that verbal violence can be as destructive as physical. Best of all, most people today no longer believe that child abuse is a problem for government agencies to solve alone; research has shown that the majority of the public now believe we can all do something to end child abuse in our communities.

As a childcare worker, your most important responsibility will be ensuring the well-being and happiness of your charges.

Abby shrugged. "That's what grownups do when they get mad."

"Does your mom hit you when she's angry?" Barbara asked, her voice gentle.

Abby pulled up her shirt and showed Barbara a black-and-blue mark across her back. "That's where she hit me with the belt last time," she said, as though she were proud of the fact. "But I didn't cry."

Barbara turned the conversation back to Abby's actions in the room. She understood now that Abby was only repeating the behaviors she had learned at home, but she made sure Abby understood that physical violence was not acceptable within their room.

The time had come for the children to leave for school; Barbara said good-bye to them and then picked up the phone. She made an appointment to meet with the school's social worker to discuss Abby's situation.

All children have the right to be safe, both at home and at school. Although our world does not always treat children fairly, Barbara wanted to be sure Abby had a chance to learn there are other alternatives to violence and anger. A referral would probably be made to Social Services, so that a *child protective worker* could get involved with Abby's family. The Before- and After-School Program, the public school, and the Department of Social Services would work together to see that Abby had a chance to learn the meaning of real justice.

Children are put on earth to be loved and cared for, so everyone has a big job to do.

—Eleanor Roosevelt

Parents and grandparents often hire childcare workers to take care of children in their own home.

RESPONSIBILITY

*Sometimes we may be confused about what
our true responsibilities really are.*

CHAPTER FIVE

Lucy Kassis was a responsible person. She wasn't afraid to work hard, and the people in her life always knew they could count on her. And when she set herself a goal, she did whatever she had to do to achieve it. So when Lucy decided to start her own childcare business, she made herself a list of what she needed to do—and then she began checking off each item as she accomplished it.

She started by taking some classes at the local community college. The classes helped her understand the regulations that applied to the childcare industry; she learned the health and safety rules that needed to be followed in order to have a licensed childcare business.

If you take care of children in your home, it's important to have safe, well-maintained playground equipment.

That summer, she spent several weeks getting her house ready to be inspected by the childcare licensing department. She had to meet 120 different regulations, ranging from having all her electrical outlets covered with childproof covers to making sure the temperature on the hot water heater was at the correct setting. Lucy made sure that her home complied with each regulation—and she was delighted when she received her official childcare license, allowing her to care for six children in her home.

Lucy had studied several books on successful childcare businesses, and she felt she was ready now to put together a program that was creative and fun, as well as safe and dependable. As a responsible person, Lucy truly cared for the parents and children she would be serving. She understood the huge commitment she was making to the parents who would trust her with their children.

But she also understood that no one was going to register their children with her unless they knew her home was a childcare option. So Lucy's next responsibility was marketing.

She soon discovered that she had a real flare for advertising. The opportunity to be creative and "sell" herself to others was both fun and exciting. At an open house she hosted, she had the chance to interact personally with parents and convince them she could offer their children the care they needed.

Being responsible means:

- your behavior shows you can be trusted.
- you deliver what you promise.
- you always do your best.
- you don't make excuses for yourself.

Puzzles and other educational toys will make your home an educational and fun place where children can spend their day.

Young children learn mainly through play. Childcare workers often make use of children's play to further their language development (through storytelling and playacting games, for instance), improve social skills (by taking turns while playing a game or working together to build a simple project out of milk cartons), and introduce science and math skills (through counting blocks, for example, or mixing paint colors).

"Do you have art as part of your program?" one mother asked.

"Of course," Lucy answered smoothly. She opened a cupboard where art supplies were neatly stacked. "I believe it's important to encourage children's creativity."

"What about music?" asked another parent.

Lucy hesitated. Truthfully, she wasn't a very musical person, and she hadn't give much thought to how she would incorporate

If you remodel your home to use as a daycare facility, you will need to have it approved by a childcare licensing department. Stairs, electrical outlets, and other hazards will need to conform to regulations.

Art supplies are a "must" for daycare facilities.

music in her program. But she betrayed none of her doubts and nodded her head with enthusiasm. "Yes, music is another vital part of a child's day. We will be having plenty of opportunities to sing and listen to music every day." She made a mental note to herself: *Get a CD player.*

The questions kept coming from the parents—and Lucy answered each query with an affirmative. "Yes, yes," she agreed, "I will provide your child with that."

"The childcare center across town puts on little plays every few months for the parents," put in one father. "Will you be doing anything like that?"

Lucy nodded again, but by this time she was no longer making mental notes to herself. She was simply agreeing with whatever the parents wanted. Once she had their children enrolled in her

Marketing Strategies for Starting Your Own Childcare Business

- Make a brochure that includes your schedule, philosophy, goals, programs, and a picture of yourself and your facility.
- Hold an open house or tour of your home. Serve guests coffee and snacks.
- Make business cards for yourself. Tell everyone you know that you are starting a childcare business and give them your cards, with extras to share.
- Advertise in the local newspaper.
- If your community zoning allows, put up a sign outside your home with your logo, name, and phone number.
- Make sure the outside of your home is as attractive as the interior.
- Leave your name and phone number with the local grade school secretary.
- Advertise with county referral agencies.
- Frame and hang any license or training certificates you possess.
- Have a list of references you can hand out to prospective parents.
- Provide nontraditional work hours. Be flexible with your opening and closing times.
- When speaking with parents and children, be involved with both of them. Allow parents a chance to see your skills with children first hand.
- Remember that responsible salespeople only market services they can really offer. Create the best service you are capable of delivering—and then be honest. If your program is truly high quality, it will help sell itself.

program, she would have time to actually determine what she could do. Right now, she decided, her only responsibility was to market herself.

Do you think she was right?

For this stage of her new career, Lucy saw being a successful salesperson as her chief responsibility. Do you think she had a still bigger responsibility, one that she had missed?

Give to the world the best you have, and the best will come back to you.

—Madeline S. Bridges

You probably wouldn't suspect that a childcare worker would need courage to do his job—but you might be surprised.

COURAGE

Courage means we're willing to pay the price of acting on our convictions.

CHAPTER SIX

A year ago, if you'd asked Washington Jones if he needed courage to do his job, he probably would have said no. After all, he ran a daycare center; he worked with little kids all day. Why would he need courage? It wasn't like he'd ever be afraid of preschoolers. Recently, though, Washington ran into a situation that demanded all the courage he had.

"I'm going to withdraw Jasmine," a mother told Washington one afternoon when she came to pick her daughter up from his center. "I don't want her here anymore."

Washington looked down at Jasmine, whose chubby hands were wrapped firmly around his leg. "What's the problem?" he asked her mother. "Jasmine's always so happy here."

Jasmine's mother pressed her lips tight together. "I need to know she's safe. I don't want her somewhere she could get sick."

Washington was bewildered. "Mrs. Robinson, the center is inspected regularly by the state. We're not exposing the children to any health hazards. Jasmine's not going to get sick from being here."

Mrs. Robinson just shook her head. "I don't want Jasmine here." She peeled Jasmine off Washington's leg and marched away. The set of her shoulders told Washington she wouldn't be coming back.

The following day, two more parents told Washington they were pulling their children out of his center. Later in the week, another parent did the same, and then another. Washington called a staff meeting to see if he could determine what was going on, but none of the workers offered him any information.

Life will present you with many opportunities to do good. To take advantage of these opportunities, you will need to learn to think before you act.

AIDS is a tragic fact of life in today's world, one that touches millions of people—including children.

After the meeting, however, Robin Curran lingered behind as the other workers left the room. "I think it's Lydia," she told Washington in a quiet voice. "The rumor must have gotten out."

"What rumor?"

"Well, it's not just a rumor." Robin looked uncomfortable. "Lydia is *HIV-positive*. She was born that way; her mother died from *AIDS* a few years ago, and her father has remarried since then. The step-mom told me when she enrolled Lydia. Lydia's not sick; she hasn't shown any symptoms yet, and she shares a home with her stepbrothers and stepsisters. None of them are HIV-positive, just Lydia. The family takes

People who value courage:

- say what's right (even when no one agrees with them).
- do the right thing (even when it's hard).
- follow their conscience (instead of the crowd).

Helping to keep young children healthy is an important part of any childcare worker's job. These workers see that children eat nutritious meals and snacks; they ensure that children have proper rest periods. They identify children who may not feel well or who show signs of emotional or developmental problems. Any problems like these should be discussed with both the childcare supervisor and the children's parents.

ordinary precautions. The step-mom made sure I understood that there's nothing to worry about."

Washington nodded. He knew that state law did not require either adults or children to reveal if they had AIDS or were HIV-positive. Workers in all helping professions, from teachers to dentists to emergency medical technicians, took "universal precautions." In other words, they assumed that anyone *might* have AIDS, and they were careful to avoid direct contact with blood or other body fluids.

Childcare workers need to be sensitive to signs that something is not right in a child's life.

As a childcare worker, you will have the chance to teach children the importance of tolerance and acceptance.

He was sad little Lydia had such a serious condition, but he was not worried she would infect others.

He knew, however, that many people would not feel comfortable around Lydia. The threat of **AIDS** is terrifying, and not everyone understands how the disease is spread. If the rumor had gotten out that Lydia was HIV-positive, that explained why so many parents were withdrawing their children from his center.

The following day, yet another parent approached Washington. He braced himself for what she would say—but instead, she handed him a sheet of paper and turned her back. The sheet of paper held a petition signed by more than 20 parents. They were asking that Lydia be removed from the daycare center so that their own children would not be placed at risk.

In some cases, childcare workers may help parents identify their children's specific needs. This may mean a referral to another agency or program, where children's needs can be adequately addressed. Early identification of children with special needs, such as those with emotional, physical, or learning disabilities, means that these children can begin receiving the treatment or intervention that will help them be more successful in the future.

Later that day, some of his workers came to Washington with their own demands that Lydia be removed. They had heard from the parents that Lydia had AIDS—and they did not want to risk being exposed to her themselves.

What should Washington do? The easiest, cheapest thing would be to simply give in to the demands of the parents and workers: he

If you decide to work as a childcare worker, you need to remember that parents are trusting you with their most valuable treasure—their children.

Financial pressures cannot be ignored. Only you can make the decision whether ethical principles should come first before financial concerns.

could ask Lydia's parents to remove their daughter from his child-care center. As much as he hated to do it, what choice did he have?

But Washington knew that Lydia's parents needed a good place to send their daughter while they went to work. They were depending on Washington to provide Lydia with the care she needed—and Washington longed for the courage to meet the needs of Lydia and her family. Still, what could he do? Without his workers, Washington could not run his business—and without children, he had no business at all. He would never have guessed that one little girl could threaten to shut down his entire childcare center.

He didn't want to lose his business; he had bills to pay, and the thought of starting a new business scared him. But something inside him told him he would be wrong to ask Lydia to leave. There had to be another option—if he could just find the courage to look for it.

Washington sucked in a deep breath. Then he picked up the phone and began making some calls. He could at least look for alternatives.

By the end of the day, Washington knew what his next step would be. He had written a letter to all the parents of children who attended his daycare center, inviting them to an informational meeting on AIDS and HIV. A doctor and a nurse at the local hospital had volunteered to speak at the meeting. They would also provide handout materials to be sent home to those parents who were unable to attend. Both the meeting and the handouts would focus on the medical facts about AIDS and HIV—how the disease was spread, how it could be avoided, what people should fear—and what they shouldn't.

Washington wasn't certain what his next step would be—or if he would even need to take another step. He knew there were no guarantees the informational meeting would convince parents that Lydia was no danger to their children. Washington was still scared. But he was determined to ignore his fear and do what he could.

To do anything in this world worth doing, we must not stand back shivering and thinking of the cold and danger, but jump in and scramble through as well as we can.

—Sydney Smith

Caring for an infant can be rewarding and fun—and it can also require more self-discipline and diligence than almost any other job.

SELF-DISCIPLINE AND DILIGENCE

No matter how diligent we may be at our work, sometimes we need enough self-discipline to ask for help.

CHAPTER SEVEN

Being diligent and self-disciplined seemed to come naturally to Renee Stuart. For as long as she could remember, she had wanted to work with children. She had always loved little kids, and she got along well with them, but she especially liked babies. As a teenager, she had many babysitting jobs, and parents were always impressed by her maturity and hard work.

So when she got a job as a nanny for three-month-old twins, Renee was delighted. Her new job meant she didn't even have to find an apartment. After she graduated from high school, she moved directly to her new suite in the Bordens' large house. The Bordens were both doctors; Dr. Meg Borden would be returning to her practice at a local

Very young children are adorable—and demanding.

hospital after her maternity leave, and Renee would take care of their daughters while the two doctors were at work.

Renee loved little Megan and Sarah—but she was surprised by how much work two little babies could make. She was constantly doing laundry, constantly changing them, constantly feeding them . . . and by the time the Bordens came home in the evening, Renee was exhausted. She was grateful to turn the babies over to their parents and relax in the peace and quiet of her suite.

Because the Bordens were doctors, however, they sometimes worked long and irregular hours. Renee hated the times when emergencies or other circumstances kept both Bordens at the hospital until early in the morning. Megan and Sarah were still too little to sleep through the night—and sometimes Renee felt as though she would lose her mind if she could not get some sleep.

Luckily, those times didn't happen very often. For the most part, Renee was still happy with her job. She enjoyed taking care of the twins, and she liked the Bordens and the chance to be a part of their home. Besides, she knew she was learning a lot about babies.

All her life, Renee had been a hard worker. She didn't back down from a job just because it was difficult, and she had always been self-disciplined enough to overcome the challenges life presented. Taking care of two babies had proved to be harder than she had ever expected—but she wasn't about to give up.

But in the middle of one dark night, Renee began to wonder if she should quit her job. She even wondered if she could make it through the night.

The Bordens had called earlier to say they would both be working late. Renee had been with the twins since seven o'clock that morning, and neither of them had slept at the same time all day. They were both *colicky*, and they were fussy and miserable. If

Babies who have learned to navigate need to be watched carefully. They are curious about everything, and they can easily break something or injure themselves.

Megan napped, Sarah cried; and if Sarah dropped off to sleep, Megan fussed until Renee picked her up. Renee was exhausted.

At midnight, Renee finally got both babies settled down in their cribs and tiptoed out of their room. She had just fallen asleep herself, when Sarah's soft wail woke her up. Renee lay still, hoping the baby would fall back asleep. Instead, she woke her sister, and Megan began to scream like a fire engine. As Sarah's sobs also increased in volume, Renee staggered out of bed.

She picked up both babies, and walked around and around the nursery, jiggling them gently in her arms. They finally quieted, and Renee eased little Sarah back into her crib. As she did so, though, Megan woke up and began to cry again.

"No!" Renee screamed almost as loudly as Megan. The baby was so startled that for an instant she was silent; then she began to wail again, and Sarah woke up and joined her.

Renee's head was hurting. She longed for sleep . . . and quiet. Her hands closed tight around Megan's little shoulders. For a few

Colicky babies may cry for hours without stopping.

seconds, she found herself wanting to shake the baby until she was quiet . . . she wanted to throw her. . .

Renee's own thoughts horrified her. She put the baby carefully in her crib and went out into the hallway. Her back against the wall, she took several long, deep breaths, trying to find the strength to go back into the nursery.

She could do it, she tried to tell herself. She didn't need to ask for help. . .

But she was afraid to trust herself to go back in that room. The babies were still crying, and their sobs made her feel guilty—but right now, she realized, she needed help. She picked up the phone and called her mother.

Renee hated to confess how desperate she felt. But when she did, her mother instantly understood. "Anyone who's taken care of babies—anyone who's honest that is—will tell you that sooner or later you feel the urge to throw the baby across the room."

Renee was both shocked and relieved to hear her mother's words.

"That's when you make sure they're not wet," her mother continued, "and they're not sick and nothing's poking them. You see if

People who value self-discipline and diligence:

- work to control their emotions, words, actions, and impulses.
- give their best in all situations.
- keep going even when the going is rough.
- are determined and patient.
- look for ways to do their work better.

And this means that sometimes, people who are self-disciplined and diligent need to know their own limitations—and ask for help when the job is too big for them!

According to the Center for the Prevention of Child Abuse, 3.3 reports of child abuse are made each year in the United States.

A fretful baby can sometimes be distracted by a toy or some other interesting object.

they're hungry or thirsty . . . and if they're still crying and your patience is all used up, you put them in their cribs where they're safe, and you shut the door until you have the strength to go back and pick them up one more time. Babies just ask too much sometimes, more than we know how to give. So you know your limits, and you keep them safe—and you ask for help when you need it."

After she hung up the phone, Renee sat for a moment longer, thinking about her mother's words. She hated to realize that as self-disciplined and diligent as she considered herself to be, two little babies had proved to be too much for her. But maybe they would have been too much for anyone. . .

Sarah and Megan were quiet now, she realized. She tiptoed into the nursery and found them sleeping peacefully. As she watched their soft, even breathing, Renee tried to think what she should do in the morning.

She had always assumed that being a diligent, self-disciplined person meant that you never gave up . . . and you never asked for help. But maybe sometimes, it took even more self-discipline to

Babies deserve to be safe and loved. Do you have the self-discipline and diligence to do the job?

admit that you couldn't keep going if you didn't have help. The only thing she had to lose, she realized, was her pride—and Sarah and Megan were too precious to put at risk simply because she was ashamed to confess she wasn't perfect.

When the Bordens came home, she decided, she would have to talk to them. She wanted to continue as their nanny, and she didn't want to leave the twins—but she also needed to tell them that on the nights when they worked late, she needed someone to help her. Taking care of two babies for 18 hours at a time was just too much for her. She was a diligent worker who loved her job—but she was self-disciplined enough to admit when she needed help.

What do you think the Bordens' reaction will be when Renee talks to them? Do you expect they will respect Renee's request—or will they decide they need someone else to look after their children? In either case, do you think Renee has made the right decision? What would you do in her place?

The difficulties and struggles of today are but the price we must pay for the accomplishments and victories of tomorrow.

—William J. H. Boetcker

Children's play is their "work," the task that helps them learn to be happy and productive adults.

CITIZENSHIP

Being a good citizen means we do what we can to make our world better for everyone.

CHAPTER EIGHT

Playing with children may seem like such a little thing to do for the world. But researchers have proven that play stimulates creativity and imagination, and allows children to expand the horizons of their world. When children pretend to be doctors, teachers, parents, or firefighters, they learn that life is full of possibilities and opportunities. They have the chance to try on lots of hats—and get a sense for which one fits them best. Play is the primary way children learn about themselves, others, and their world. Through play, children develop the physical, mental, social, emotional, and creative skills needed for life.

Play is an important part of any childcare worker's job—but so are the character traits we've already discussed in this book—integrity, compassion, responsibility, courage, and diligence. Parents trust childcare workers with that which is most precious to them—their children. They count on childcare workers to be people of character, people they can trust to help them raise their children.

A century ago, most childcare occurred in the home; if circumstances prevented mothers and fathers from caring for their children themselves, then older siblings or grandparents often watched over the little ones. But in today's world, things have changed. Most families need two incomes, and extended families no longer live in one household or even in the same community. This means that mothers and fathers need to find someone outside their family, someone they can trust, to care for their children.

Each child is a piece of our world's future.

As a result, childcare workers not only provide a service to families—they also enable all the other jobs in a community to take place. After all, without someone to watch their children, mothers and fathers could not be teachers and doctors, store clerks and business managers, factory workers and farmers.

Our society is a web of people, all working together to build the human community. Since children are our future, the people who care for them are an essential part of this web. They are good citizens who provide a much-needed service to the entire community.

Many programs around the country honor childcare workers for the citizenship they demonstrate through their jobs. For instance, the Providian Financial Corporation (now part of Washington Mutual, Inc.) set up the Excellence in Service to Children Awards program in 2000. These awards recognized the hard work and dedication of people int he community who were willing to devote themselves every day to children. Honorees were selected from hundreds of

According to the Character Counts Coalition, citizenship is:

- playing by the rules.
- obeying the law.
- doing your share.
- respecting authority.
- keeping informed about current events.
- voting.
- protecting your neighbors and community.
- paying your taxes.
- giving to others in your community who are in need.
- volunteering to help.

Citizenship also means protecting the future by. . .

- caring for the environment,
- conserving natural resources,
- and doing all that we can to ensure that children in our community grow up safe, happy, and healthy.

Childcare workers who help children learn and be happy are good citizens who contribute to the well-being of their entire communities.

nominations made by parents and peers; they were individuals who work in childcare programs, or who opened their homes to children. The State of Delaware also sponsors the Governor's Awards for Excellence in Early Care and Education, and the Child Care Services Association in Chapel Hill, North Carolina, presents awards to dedicated childcare workers. In Canada, the Association of Canadian Community Colleges (ACCC) has its own award program.

In 2000, the ACCC winner was Pat Tretjack. As the supervisor of the Trafalgar Road Childcare Centre, Pat is the kind of person that both adults and children remember long after they come in contact with her. She believes in bringing generations together, allowing children and volunteer "grandparents" the chance to interact and benefit from each other. Her role as the Centre's supervisor means that she blends management skills with those of early childhood educator. As a result, the staff, the children, and the entire community benefits. She is truly a good citizen, a valuable resource for her society.

Being a person of character means you choose to do the right thing at home, at work, and in the community. It is a balancing act of being simultaneously trusting, respectful, responsible, fair and caring while being a good citizen, says Michael Josephson, the founder of the Josephson Institute of Ethics in Marina del Rey. At its most difficult, Josephson warns, being ethical means making choices that may cost money, a job, or a friend. "The wonderful thing about ethics is it's purely about choices," Josephson said. "You can be a horrible person yesterday and a better person today."

This worker in an after-school program is providing his community with a vital service.

One of the most powerful ways to make a difference in your community is by influencing the life of a child.

Women Who Made a Difference in Their Communities

- In the 1940s, Jeannette Watson was given the nickname "Mrs. Early Childhood Education of Texas" because she began a childcare center that created many innovative programs for children and their families.
- Mozelle Core operated childcare centers in Nashville, Tennessee, and inspired generations of early childhood professionals to always give high quality childcare.
- Polly Greenberg worked hard to make the **Head Start** program a success in America. She was part of a team that encouraged parent participation in this preschool program.

Sometimes we think being a good citizen means only that we do the obvious things to help our country—things like voting or paying our taxes. But what better way is there to help our country than to protect and care for its future—our children?

Each citizen should play his part in the community according to his individual gifts.

—Plato

As a childcare worker, you may care for a child like this in a nursery school or preschool.

CAREER OPPORTUNITIES

*Life is full of all sorts of wonderful
opportunities ... and the best ones
usually have nothing to do with
money or prestige.*

CHAPTER NINE

As a childcare worker, you may do your job in a childcare center, nursery school, preschool, public school, or private household. Whatever the setting, you will play an important role in many families. While parents are at work or unable to care for their children for other reasons, you will be the person responsible for these small but very important people. You will not only have the opportunity to keep them safe and healthy; you will also have the chance to teach them how to get along better with others; you will have many occasions when you can stimulate their imaginations and encourage their emotional and intellectual growth. You will help children explore their interests and develop their independence; you will have the opportunity to nurture their self-esteem and help them become happy, healthy members of our world.

Childcare workers held about 1.3 million jobs in 2010. Twenty-two percent worked in child day care services, 15 percent in private households, and 11 percent in schools. A very small percentage of private industries operate onsite childcare centers for the children of their employees.

Turnover in this occupation is high. Many childcare workers leave the occupation temporarily to fulfill their own family responsibilities; some leave permanently because they have chosen to further their education or because they are interested in pursuing other professional opportunities. Long hours, low pay, and stressful conditions are all too common in this career, which means that many workers will seek other career alternatives. This turnover, however, has a positive side as well: new jobs are constantly opening

Childcare workers may help children explore the natural world.

for those who are looking to enter this field.

As a result, the number of jobs in the childcare industry is expected to grow 20 percent between 2010 and 2020. (Jobs for all industries combined are only expected to grow by 14 percent.) This rising demand for childcare workers reflects the increasing number of women in the workforce.

Unfortunately, childcare workers' hourly earnings tend to be less than the average for all other industries combined. The hourly pay rate ranges between $7.65 and $14.08, and average $9.28 per hour (compared to $16.27, which is the hourly average for all other industries). A large portion of childcare workers—39 percent—work part-time. Employee

Whatever career you choose, chances are good that you will one day be a childcare worker— a parent. If you have children of your own, you will need the skills—and the character qualities—that any professional childcare worker requires. Your children will learn by **modeling** your behavior. As they imitate you, what character traits will they develop?

How Did I Live Today?

Thomas Shanks, S.J., Ph.D. of the Markkula Center for Applied Ethics, recommends that everyone ask themselves these five questions at the end of the day.

- Did I practice any virtues (e.g., integrity, honesty, compassion)?
- Did I do more good than harm?
- Did I treat others with dignity and respect?
- Was I fair and just?
- Was my community better because I was in it? Was I better because I was in my community?

Whatever other career you may choose, if one day you become a parent, you will also be a childcare worker.

benefits are often minimal as well. Many childcare centers offer their staff no healthcare benefits—but many centers do allow employees' children to attend for free. Nonprofit and religious childcare centers tend to pay better and have more generous benefit packages than for-profit childcare centers. The more education a childcare worker has, the more he or she is likely to be paid.

Because the need for quality childcare is such a real and growing aspect of our society, politicians and social activists have made childcare one of today's most talked-about careers. Hopefully, the increased attention will mean that salaries and working conditions will improve during the next decade. Federal and state governments are increasingly involved in promoting and funding childcare services. Head Start and other national childcare programs have been granted increased funding from the federal government, and many state governments are implementing mandatory preschool programs for four-year-olds. Welfare reform legislation that requires more welfare recipients to work could also contribute to an increased government awareness of the demand for childcare services.

Children are not just demanding little people who must be kept clean and amused. In a very real way, they are our world's future. When you care for them with integrity, respect, fairness, courage, responsibility, and diligence, you are also caring for the future. You are a good citizen in the truest sense of the word, for you are helping to grow tomorrow's citizens.

If you are looking for a job as a childcare worker, you may find a checklist like this one helpful in determining the best location to work:

- How does the childcare center promote children's health and nutritional needs?
- Are all areas cleaned regularly?
- Are toys and materials disinfected on a regular basis?
- Do caregivers wash hands after diapering, toileting, blowing noses, and before handling food?
- Are medications stored out of the reach of children and ad ministered properly?
- Does the facility serve nutritious snacks and meals? Are menus posted?
- Do caregivers sit with children at mealtimes to model appropriate manners, interactions, nutritious choices, and the positive social nature of mealtimes?
- Is positive guidance used as the guiding philosophy in the classroom?
- Are disruptive reactions responded to quickly and with understanding to maintain a positive atmosphere in the classroom?

Childcare is never routine. New activities and challenges mark each day. As you watch children grow, learn, and gain new skills, you will have the satisfaction of knowing you are truly making a difference in our world.

- Do teacher/child ratios meet or exceed state requirements?
- Are there well-defined written emergency procedures in place?
- Are children encouraged to challenge themselves and try new things?
- Do children receive positive reinforcement for accomplishing goals?
- Do the children in the program seem relaxed and happy?
- Are children offered a variety of meaningful learning choices throughout the day?
- Are caregivers supported by professional resource people, training, and materials?
- Are there activities and learning programs that are developmentally appropriate and geared to the needs of children of different ages, abilities, and learning styles?
- Is there frequent and consistent communication between staff and parents regarding the developmental progress of children, as well as regularly scheduled conferences?

Keep true, never be ashamed of doing right; decide on what you think is right and stick to it.

—George Eliot

Further Reading

Connell, Linda H. *The Childcare Answer Book*. Naperville, Ill.: Sphinx Publishing, 2005.

Johnson, Jeff A. *Finding Your Smile Again: A Child Care Professional's Guide to Reducing Stress and Avoiding Burnout*. St. Paul, Minn: Redleaf Press, 2007.

Musial, Tina. *How to Open & Operate a Financially Successful Child Care Service*. Ocala, Fla.: Atlantic Publishing Group, Inc., 2007.

Josephson, Michael S. and Wes Hanson, editors. *The Power of Character*. Bloomington, Ind.: Unlimited Press, 2004.

Kidder, Rushworth M. *How Good People Make Tough Choices*. New York: HarperCollins, 2009.

For More Information

Canadian Child Care Federation
www.cccf-fcsge.ca

Character Education Network
www.charactered.net

Josephson Institute of Ethics
www.josephsoninstitute.org

The National Association of Child Care Professionals
www.naccp.org/index.cfm

The National Association for the Education of Young Children
www.naeyc.org

The National Association for Family Child Care
www.nafcc.org

Publisher's Note:
The websites on this page were active at the time of publication. The publisher is not responsible for websites that have changed their address or discontinued operation since the date of publication. The publisher will review and update the websites upon each reprint.

Glossary

Affiliates Closely associated organizations.

AIDS Acquired immunodeficiency syndrome; a disease of the human immune system caused by HIV; it makes victims susceptible to other life-threatening diseases.

Associate's degree A two-year degree.

Child protective worker A person employed by the Department of Social Services who works with children and their families where abuse or the risk of abuse is present.

Colicky Having abdominal pain, a condition common to young babies.

Ethical dilemmas Situations where a person must make a choice about what is right and what is wrong.

Head Start A preschool program funded by the federal government, intended to help prevent children from having later problems in school.

HIV-positive Possessing the virus that causes AIDS; HIV infects and destroys helper T cells in the immune system. A person can be HIV-positive without yet being sick with AIDS.

Modeling Imitating another's behavior.

Pediatrician A physician who specializes in treating children.

Private Funded by an individual or an institution.

Public Funded by the entire community, usually through taxes.

Index

About the Author & Consultants

Ellyn Sanna has authored more than 50 books, including adult non-fiction, novels, young adult biographies, and gift books.

Ernestine G. Riggs is an associate professor at Loyola University Chicago. She has been involved in the field of education for more than forty years and has a diverse background in teaching and administration. Riggs was selected as one of the Outstanding Elementary Teachers of America by the United States Department of Defense Overseas Schools in 1974. She is the coauthor of *Beyond Rhetoric and Rainbows: A Journey to the Place Where Learning Lives*, *Helping Middle and High School Readers: Teaching and Learning Strategies Across the Curriculum*, and several journal articles. She is also co-featured in the video *Ensuring Success for "Low Yield" Students: Building Lives and Molding Futures*. In the summer of 2007, Riggs was invited to present a précis of the research on conation at the prestigious Oxford Round Table in Oxford, England. Riggs is a frequent presenter at local, district, national, and international conferences.

Cheryl R. Gholar has been a teacher, counselor, and administrator in public schools and worked in postsecondary education for more than thirty years. She is associate director of the Professional Development Consortium. Gholar is coauthor of *Beyond Rhetoric and Rainbows: A Journey to the Place Where Learning Lives*. She is also co-featured in the video *Ensuring Success for "Low Yield" Students: Building Lives and Molding Futures*. She is published in *Vitae Scholasticae*, *Black Issues in Higher Education*, *The Journal of Staff Development*, *Careers With Character*, and more. Gholar's awards include Educator of the Year; Phi Delta Kappa; Those Who Excel; Oppenheimer Family Foundation; Outstanding Teacher, Chicago Region PTA; and Outstanding Contributions to The Department of Character Education, Chicago Public Schools.

MAY 2014

Northport-East Northport Public Library

To view your patron record from a computer, click on
the Library's homepage: **www.nenpl.org**

You may:
- request an item be placed on hold
- renew an item that is overdue
- view titles and due dates checked out on your card
- view your own outstanding fines

151 Laurel Avenue
Northport, NY 11768
631-261-6930